Native American
Festivals and Ceremonies

JENNA GLATZER

Senior Consulting Editor Dr. Troy Johnson
Professor of History and American Indian Studies
California State University

MASON CREST PUBLISHERS • PHILADELPHIA

NATIVE AMERICAN LIFE

NATIVE AMERICAN LIFE

Europeans and Native Americans

Homes of the Native Americans

Hunting with the Native Americans

Native American Confederacies

Native American Cooking

Native American Family Life

Native American Festivals and Ceremonies

Native American Horsemanship

Native American Languages

Native American Medicine

Native American Religions

Native American Rivalries

Native American Sports and Games

Native American Tools and Weapons

What the Native Americans Wore

Native American
Festivals and Ceremonies

JENNA GLATZER

Senior Consulting Editor Dr. Troy Johnson
Professor of History and American Indian Studies
California State University

MASON CREST PUBLISHERS • PHILADELPHIA

NATIVE AMERICAN LIFE

This book is dedicated to Paul Glatzer (the best brother in the world) and Marie Chieffo, because she never forgets a promise!

Mason Crest Publishers
370 Reed Road
Broomall, PA 19008
www.masoncrest.com

3 5 7 9 8 6 4 2

Library of Congress Cataloging-in-Publication Data

Glatzer, Jenna.
   Native American festivals and ceremonies / Jenna Glatzer.
      p.   cm. — (Native American life)
Summary: Describes some of the ceremonies and festivals that Native
American peoples use to celebrate special occasions, give thanks,
remember their dead, and communicate with spirits.
Includes bibliographical references and index.
   ISBN 1-59084-123-9
1. Indians—Rites and ceremonies—Juvenile literature.
2. Indians—Social life and customs—Juvenile literature.
3. Festivals—America—Juvenile literature. [1. Indians of North
America—Rites and ceremonies. 2. Indians—Rites and ceremonies.
3. Indians of North America—Social life and customs.
4. Indians—Social life and customs.] I. Title. II. Series.
E59.R38 G557 2002
306.4'08'97—dc21
                                                    2002023134

Table of Contents

Introduction: Dr. Troy Johnson 6

1 Native American Festivals 9

2 Festivals of the Northeast.......................................15

3 Festivals of the Southeast...23

4 Ceremonies of the Southwest and West....................................31

5 Central and South American Festivals 43

6 Festivals of the North 49

Chronology..56

Glossary 58

Further Reading...60

Internet Resources 61

Index..62

Introduction

For hundreds of years the dominant image of the Native American has been that of a stoic warrior, often wearing a full-length eagle feather headdress, riding a horse in pursuit of the buffalo, or perhaps surrounding some unfortunate wagon train filled with innocent west-bound American settlers. Unfortunately there has been little written or made available to the general public to dispel this erroneous generalization. This misrepresentation has resulted in an image of native people that has been translated into books, movies, and television programs that have done little to look deeply into the native worldview, cosmology, and daily life. Not until the 1990 movie *Dances with Wolves* were native people portrayed as having a human persona. For the first time, native people could express humor, sorrow, love, hate, peace, and warfare. For the first time native people could express themselves in words other than "ugh" or "Yes, Kemo Sabe." This series has been written to provide a more accurate and encompassing journey into the world of the Native Americans.

When studying the native world of the Americas, it is extremely important to understand that there are few "universals" that apply across tribal boundaries. With over 500 nations and 300 language groups the worlds of the Native Americans were diverse. The traditions of one group may or may not have been shared by neighboring groups. Sports, games, dance, subsistence patterns, clothing, and religion differed—greatly in some instances. And although nearly all native groups observed festivals and ceremonies necessary to insure the renewal of their worlds, these too varied greatly.

Of equal importance to the breaking down of old myopic and stereotypic images is that the authors in this series credit Native

Americans with a sense of agency. Contrary to the views held by the Europeans who came to North and South America and established the United States, Canada, Mexico, and other nations, some Native American tribes had sophisticated political and governing structures—that of the member nations of the Iroquois League, for example. Europeans at first denied that native people had religions but rather "worshiped the devil," and demanded that Native Americans abandon their religions for the Christian worldview. The readers of this series will learn that native people had well-established religions, led by both men and women, long before the European invasion began in the 16th and 17th centuries.

Gender roles also come under scrutiny in this series. European settlers in the northeastern area of the present-day United States found it appalling that native women were "treated as drudges" and forced to do the men's work in the agricultural fields. They failed to understand, as the reader will see, that among this group the women owned the fields and scheduled the harvests. Europeans also failed to understand that Iroquois men were diplomats and controlled over one million square miles of fur-trapping area. While Iroquois men sat at the governing council, Iroquois clan matrons caucused with tribal members and told the men how to vote.

These are small examples of the material contained in this important series. The reader is encouraged to use the extended bibliographies provided with each book to expand his or her area of specific interest.

Dr. Troy Johnson
Professor of History and American Indian Studies
California State University

Cherokee Indians perform a traditional dance during a modern-day powwow. The native inhabitants of North and South America often danced at their ceremonies and festivals; the dances had different purposes, such as giving the dancers strength for a hunt or protection during battle.

1 Native American Festivals

Native Americans had many different kinds of festivals and ceremonies to honor different events, seasons, people, places, and elements of nature. Today, many of these celebrations still exist in Native American communities. Some have been lost over the years, but we can learn a lot about Native American peoples by studying these traditions: what was important to the people and what they hoped, believed, feared, and prayed for.

Festivals and ceremonies were held for different reasons. Usually, an event was meant to give thanks for good things (like successful hunts and harvests), to mark an important change in someone's life (like when boys and girls began adulthood), or to communicate with the spirits (asking them to bring rain or heal sick people, for instance). A ceremony was a holy, spiritual event, while a festival was less formal and more social. There were some sacred ceremonies only for women or only for men.

These festivals and ceremonies were colorful and exciting. Different tribes had different kinds of occasions, but they all shared things in common. For example, participants wore fancy clothing, often sang, danced, and played instruments, feasted on wonderful meals, held contests, smoked tobacco, and gave gifts. Keeping traditions alive was important to the Native Americans. Thus, there were certain "rules" the Native Americans followed, depending on the type of event. These rules were passed down from parents to children and family to family so they could remember the ways to celebrate, give thanks, remember the dead, and communicate with spirits.

What kind of holidays do you celebrate? You can probably name plenty of days your family celebrates—things like birthdays, weddings, and religious holidays. But have you ever thought about having a special party when the corn is ripe?

The Native Americans did. They called it the Green Corn Ceremony, and it was a big event for many tribes every summer. Parents and children would eagerly wait for the time when the corn had grown high enough and was almost ready to eat. Then they would gather together and throw a big celebration lasting almost a week.

That wasn't unusual for Native Americans. Many of their festivals and ceremonies lasted for several days. There were different traditions each day of the celebration. The activities often began before the sun rose and didn't end until late at night. Even young children were expected to participate, so parents would wake them early to join the activities.

Not all of the festivals and ceremonies were fun, either. Some of them involved physical torture for the warriors or scary experiences for the children. Several of the events were a test of endurance, stamina, and strength. To refuse to participate in these events could cause a person to lose *status* in the eyes of the tribe.

However, most Native Americans looked forward to the festivals and ceremonies, which were usually about celebrating, bringing families together, appreciating life, and having a good time.

The elaborate clothing Native Americans wore

A young man wears a beaded headband, feathered headdress, and face paint. Members of Native American tribes created special, colorful clothing that they wore for their festivals and special occasions. This clothing is called regalia.

during important events is known as *regalia*, never as "costumes."
There are different rules and traditions regarding regalia for various
occasions and in different areas. For example, certain types of feathers,
colors, beads, animal skins, or other materials are appropriate for specific
dances and specific tribes. Participants today may spend hundreds, or
even thousands, of dollars on their regalia, which are all unique and
made by hand.

Today, there are a few festivals and ceremonies that non-natives can
attend, but most ceremonies are only for Native Americans. Sometimes,
Native Americans will invite a non-native friend to join in, but this is
a special honor. You can't ask to participate—that's like knocking on
someone's door and asking if you can come to dinner at their house.
Instead, you must wait for an invitation.

This has happened, in part, because Native Americans are upset
that non-natives have exploited their customs. Sometimes, non-natives
will learn about certain native ceremonies and practices, then lead
their own groups teaching about "native ways." This is insulting
because many Native American ceremonies are sacred and cannot be

taken out of context. There are many cases of a non-native person selling classes or charging membership fees to ceremonies they claim are authentic. For this reason, it may take time for a non-native to gain the trust needed to earn an invitation to ceremonies. 𝕊

The dances done during festivals had various meanings, and sometimes led to other dances or ceremonies with different meanings. For example, the four Native Americans in this photograph are performing a Grass Dance. The Indians of the Great Plains originally did this dance in order to flatten the tall grass before a ceremony.

A group of Mandan hunters perform a buffalo dance
in this painting from the mid-19th century. The
dancers hold their weapons—bows, shields, and long
spears—and wear buffalo-skin masks on their heads.
The dance was believed to summon the buffalo
herds. When killed, the animals would provide the
Mandan tribe with food, clothing, and shelter.

2 Festivals of the Northeast

The religious leaders (**shamans**) were in charge of the ceremonies, and they often had special areas of power. Some might be experts in healing, others in divining. With the help of spirits, they would attempt to pull sicknesses out of a person's body by blowing or sucking them out and chanting. Shamans could be men or women. They were generally older people, and they were highly respected.

The Iroquois (including the Cayuga, Mohawk, Oneida, Onondaga, and Seneca) had two important ceremonies: Midwinter and the Green Corn Ceremony. Midwinter, held in January or February each year, lasted over a week and celebrated the new year. It was a time for thanks and forgiveness, paying attention to dreams, and for starting new fires that would burn for the rest of the year. In Seneca tribes, messengers known as "Big Heads" would stir ashes with a big paddle, visiting each house to announce the start of the ritual. Traditionally, a white dog, symbolizing purity, would be sacrificed at the beginning of the ceremony and hung from a pole covered in red paint. The dog's body would later be burned. For days, people would concentrate on dream renewal and fulfillment.

The third day of Midwinter was something like Halloween. Groups of children walked though the village, guarded by an elderly woman, singing and dancing in return for "treats" of tobacco. If they didn't get a present, they could take whatever they wanted. Then came the games and dances, ending with the Four Sacred Rituals, which included the Feather Dance, Thanksgiving Dance, Personal Chant, and Bowl Game.

The Green Corn Ceremony, which was celebrated by many different tribes, including the Iroquois, was held when the corn was ripe for harvest. It was forbidden to pick corn before the ceremony. Instead, people had to rely on leftover corn from the last season. They would bring freshly picked corn to the ceremony to share with other families.

The Iroquois had lots of other festivals, too, mostly dedicated to nature. These included the Maple, Strawberry, Bean, Thunder, Moon, and Sun ceremonies. After the rituals there were feasts, although sometimes people didn't stay and eat at the ceremony. Instead, they would take the food home with them.

The Cayugas had many individual rituals to help people stay healthy and lucky. When someone died, he or she was buried in a seated position with food and tools. Ten days later, a ceremony was held. If a chief died, the *condolence* ceremony was designed to mourn the loss and to bring in a new chief.

This was different from the funeral ceremony of the Kickapoo of Michigan, Ohio, and Wisconsin (and later, Illinois and Kansas). Their dead were buried in travel clothes with even more goods: spoons, tobacco, food, and water. Funerals included feasts, singing, prayer, and silence. After someone died, people in the village left for four days, then came

NATIVE AMERICAN LIFE

back and often held an adoption ceremony. (When someone died, someone else could be "adopted" to replace the dead person.)

Mourning practices differed among tribes as well. Some groups would cut their hair or blacken their faces. In the Shawnee tribes, a replacement ceremony was common. In this ceremony a woman could formally choose a new husband to replace a husband who had died. This happened about a year after her original husband's death.

An American artist named George Catlin made this drawing of Native Americans performing the Green Corn Ceremony. This summer ritual was the most sacred time of the year for many tribes of the southeast.

Many ceremonies surrounded children and adolescents. For example, several tribes had a feast to celebrate a boy's first kill during a hunt. Most also had ceremonies for male and female puberty, when boys and girls were making the transition to adulthood.

A common practice among most native tribes was the "vision quest." Although this could take place at later times, most boys around the age of puberty were expected to *fast* and then go on an isolated quest to find a spiritual guide to help them for the rest of their lives. They might have meaningful visions or dreams during the quest.

Initiates of the Midewiwin society kept secret records in the form of pictures on birch bark scrolls.

Members of the Fox tribe, which lived in Wisconsin, Illinois, and Iowa, thought the vision quests were extremely important for boys. Those boys who had successful quests formed a medicine pack and would perform in two ceremonies every year.

There were other kinds of medicine groups in other tribes. The False Face Society, an important part of many northeastern tribes, wore wooden masks as they conducted ceremonies. Sick people could ask for help from the False Face Society. They usually used instruments, like rattles and drums, as well as tobacco in their healing rituals. To attract good spirits, the Wyandotte of the St. Lawrence River Valley held a Dance of the Fire. During this ritual, participants had to touch boiling water and burning coals or stones.

The most important Wyandotte ceremony was the Feast of the Dead, held once every 10 years. Family members would wrap bones for burial in a common grave, then tell stories, feast, give gifts, and play games to honor the dead. Algonquians, who lived in Ontario and Quebec, Canada, had a Feast of the Dead ceremony each year, which included a war dance. They invited guests to watch, and the host didn't eat while visitors were present.

Members of the False Face Society had to make their own masks, or they could hire another member of the False Face Society to carve the mask for them. They would search through the woods until they found a tree (usually basswood) whose spirit "spoke" to them. They would then build a fire, offer tobacco, and cut out a section of the living tree to make the mask.

The Narragansett people of Rhode Island changed their names several times throughout their lives during ceremonies. They also burned all of their material belongings in a yearly ceremony.

The "Midewiwin," or Medicine Dance, probably arose in the 1600s because of the high death rates due to disease. Native Americans believed that sickness and disease came from the supernatural, therefore, they turned to the spirits to cure them, too. For the Anishinabe groups, who lived in what is now present-day Ontario, Canada, dreams were important, and in order to become a member of the Midewiwin curing society, a person had to report that he or she was having specific kinds of dreams or visions. Then, the man or woman paid a fee and followed instructions, waiting to find out if he or she would be accepted. During a secret yearly meeting,

19

NATIVE AMERICAN LIFE

Members of the Iroquois False Face Society wore wooden masks like this one while performing religious or healing rituals. In spring and fall they went from house to house, shaking turtle-shell rattles and chanting to drive away the evil spirits that caused sickness.

the new members would be chosen and injected with a sacred shell to gain spiritual powers. After this, they would wear medicine bags around their necks. They were well respected, but they were not considered shamans.

The Shawnees had a Spring Bread Dance to ask for a good harvest and a Fall Bread Dance to express their gratitude for the harvest and ask for a good hunting season. They also had a War Dance in August. For as long as they lived, unless they misbehaved, the same 12 men hunted and the same 12 women cooked the feasts for these ceremonies.

Bears were significant in many festivals and ceremonies. The Lenni Len´pe tribes (part of the Algonquian tribes) had food-related ceremonies like the Iroquois, but their most important yearly festival was the bear sacrifice each winter. Bears were *revered* in the Anishinabe tribes, too, and they also had a sacred bear ceremony. The Micmac of Quebec and the Maritime provinces believed bears could change themselves into other kinds of creatures.

The Delawares, part of the Len´pe tribes, had a Big House Ceremony every fall, which lasted about a week, and included storytelling, singing, dancing, and feasting. During the 19th century, they also held Grease Drinking ceremonies. Participants would drink the grease of a bear or hog and pour some of it into a fire in the hopes that great visions would come to them.

3 Festivals of the Southeast

The Black Drink Ceremony was held by the Choctaw, Creek, and Cherokee tribes. (Some called it the "white drink" to represent purity, or the color of the foam on top of the drink.) The tribes made a drink full of caffeine and served it in a **conch** shell or pottery bowl. In normal quantities, this could act like coffee, giving an extra boost of energy. But in large quantities, it would make people vomit and sweat heavily. This was supposed to cleanse their bodies and minds to make them pure. Alabamas began almost all of their ceremonies and councils with a "black drink" tea.

This Crow medicine bundle was made by wrapping an eagle's body in cloth. Straps were attached so it could be suspended during rituals. The eagle was chosen because it was seen in a vision by the creator of the bundle. Native Americans believed the eagle was an animal of great power.

During the Green Corn Ceremony (also known as *itse selu,* or Busk), all of the tribes in this area did some "spring cleaning," making sure houses and common areas were neat and clean. The ceremony included purification rituals, meant to cleanse the body and the mind. All household fires were put out, and a high priest would light a new main fire. People would use the main fire to light new fires for their homes. Some tribes also held this ceremony for the forgiveness of crimes. The Cherokees held this ceremony for four days, when the last corn crop had ripened. After sundown dances had finished, storytelling would begin. This was a favorite part of the ceremony for children.

Children in Seminole families look forward to this ceremony today. Their families drive to swamplands in the Florida Everglades to meet other Seminole families for the event. Every afternoon during the celebration, they get together to play Seminole ball. In this game, children use rackets made out of branches to catch and throw a deerskin ball. The object is to hit the ball into a pole in the middle. Each time a team hits the pole, they make a mark on the pole to keep score.

Another important part of the ritual for the Seminoles is the medicine bundle. The tribe believes that this bundle holds magic powers, and they fear that the tribe will die if anything bad happens to it. Therefore, it is hidden in a secret spot in the swamp, and only the medicine man is allowed to touch it. Several times throughout the Green Corn Ceremony, the medicine man opens the bundle to make sure all of the contents are safely in place. Inside are stones, powder, bones, snake fangs, and other items. Men and women perform several dances around the bundle, honoring different animals. Then the medicine man goes back into the swamps to hide the bundle again until the following year.

During ceremonies, this medicine bundle was opened and
women danced with the weasel skins inside. This was believed
to ensure the abundance of the tribe's crop of tobacco, as
well as the fertility and growth of the tribe as a whole.

This painting shows members of
a Choctaw tribe participating in
a traditional ball game. Sports
and games were often important
elements of Native American
ceremonies.

For Chickasaw ceremonies, two head priests, known as *hopaye,* led the rituals. They wore special clothes and interpreted spiritual matters. Village men painted their faces during ceremonies. When someone died, his or her face would be painted, too. They had elaborate ceremonies for the dead, burying them in sitting positions in graves under homes. For three days after someone died, there were no social activities in the village.

Chickasaws danced both for fun and for spiritual purposes. Today, they have an annual festival each fall, with traditional foods like cracked corn, pork, and poke greens.

Lacrosse and other sports and games were important to tribes in the southeast. For some, sports included ceremonies and rituals involving gambling and tobacco. Days before a lacrosse game, Choctaws would conduct ceremonies. Shamans would help the players by boosting their spiritual power to help them win. Both the sport and the gambling beforehand were dangerous businesses; the gambling might leave a person broke financially, and the lacrosse might leave a person with broken bones. There weren't many rules, and the game was often played to settle arguments.

Tobacco was an important part of almost all public ceremonies in the southeast. Medicine societies used tobacco juices and teas to cure sickness and ease insect bites. Tribal councils smoked tobacco before discussing war matters. Creeks scattered it around new houses to keep ghosts away. Native Americans saw tobacco as a spiritual tool; the smoke was a prayer that was going up to the Great Spirit. They

27

NATIVE AMERICAN LIFE

smoked it to keep peace, change the weather, cure illness, and more. When European settlers arrived, they began selling tobacco for profit, which was considered a great insult to the natives.

When a Choctaw died, his or her head was painted red, and an animal might be sacrificed to travel with the person to the land of the dead. At certain times throughout the day, there were "official" times for mourning and crying. The Choctaw even paid some people to mourn for them. Afterwards, the dead person's house was burned down, and the body was left out to decompose. Later, someone would scrape off any leftover flesh and return the bones to the person's family.

In the Natchez tribe (which no longer exists), people had different ranks according to whether they were nobles or commoners. Nobles had to marry commoners (called "stinkards"), and when a noble died, his or her spouse would be sacrificed, too, along with any servants. They were supposed to provide the deceased with company into the afterlife. The noble would be laid out on a platform after death, and his house would be burned. Commoners would usually be buried in the ground. It was believed that if a person behaved well on earth, he or she would be rewarded in the afterlife. If a person behaved badly, he or she would wind up in torment, surrounded by mosquitoes and eating spoiled fish.

Tuscaroras also had different burial ceremonies depending on the person's social rank. A higher-ranking person would command a more expensive and complex burial. Mourners would paint their faces black and visit the dead in a special hut for the first day. Then, the deceased would be wrapped in blankets and mats, and a shaman would deliver a long funeral speech. Villagers would build a house around the grave. The bodies of chiefs would be removed later, so their bones could be cleaned, wrapped in deerskins, and buried next to the bones of other past chiefs.

In Chickasaw tribes, it was not acceptable for anyone to refer to dead people directly by name, as it was felt that this would draw the dead person's ghost to whoever said the name.

29

The Chitimachas had a six-day Midsummer ceremony, held in a small temple. Young men were initiated as adults during this ceremony, and they were expected to fast and dance until they wore themselves out. They also had interesting customs surrounding deaths. It is thought that the tribes had "Buzzard Men" who would take a dead body, take off all the flesh, and give the clean bones back to the deceased person's family for burial. They also held ceremonies when a war chief's bones were buried. 𝕊

NATIVE AMERICAN LIFE

The Ghost Dance started among the Sioux around 1889, but the ritual soon spread throughout the Native American tribes of the West. It was centered on a belief that through performing the dance, the buffalo would return, as would the spirits of dead warriors, who would help force the white men to leave tribal lands. Some of the dancers wore special, colorfully decorated shirts, called Ghost Shirts. They believed these would protect them against bullets. However, a tragic clash at Wounded Knee Creek proved this idea to be false. In December 1890 a group of 350 Sioux camped at Wounded Knee Creek was attacked by the U.S. Cavalry, and hundreds of unarmed men, women, and children were massacred.

4 Ceremonies of the Southwest and West

In desert areas, rain is rare, but it is important for crops, livestock, and people. The Zuñis of New Mexico had many chants and dances to ask the spirits to bring rain. Shakalo is the Zuñi name for the messengers-for-rain spirits, so they had an important celebration every winter known as the Shakalo Festival. The Zuñis prepared for this all year long, and the men who were chosen as spirit dancers went off to hidden areas to practice their chants and dances.

Six of them were the Shakalo dancers, who wore huge masks with feathers and working beaks. They didn't wear the masks on their faces; instead, they held the mask on a tall pole, and the giant skirts of the masks covered their whole bodies.

Right before the festival, the men would repaint their colorful masks. People would touch up their homes, or even build new ones, in preparation for the festival. It was an honor to have one of the Shakalo dancers visit your home. The dancers would dance all night until dawn, and they were careful to perform the dance steps perfectly. If they did not do this, they were afraid it would bring the tribe bad luck.

The Navajo had two main ceremonies, but they were quite different from one another. The Blessing Way Ceremony was used to bring good luck and protection. It could be used for a number of different reasons: for example, to help childbirth, protect livestock, increase wealth, or bless a marriage. The leader of a Blessing Way Ceremony needed a special bundle that contained stones and soil from sacred mountains to perform the ritual.

The Enemy Way Ceremony was meant to protect warriors from the ghosts of men they had killed. Singers and leaders held parts of the ceremony in different places over several days.

Starting in the Great Basin area in 1889 and then spreading to other groups in the west, a Ghost Dance was held to get white people out of Native American land and to bring their native ancestors back to life. Participants believed they were bulletproof and safe from harm because they wore special protective shirts.

The Hupas of California built large houses just for ceremonies. They held a Brush Ceremony for healing, which is still practiced today. They also had an Acorn Ceremony each fall. Women weren't allowed to participate, except to grind the acorns for the ceremony.

The Wiyot would hold special dances when a child was sick (the Brush Dance) or when an enemy was killed (Victory Dances). Wiyot women were allowed to dance in the Victory Dances, which was unusual—most tribes wouldn't let women join in this kind of dance. They also had an unusual version of the World Renewal Festival,

A 13-year-old Hopi boy named Smiling Sun has his hair braided in this photograph from the 1940s. The braid will be cut off during a ceremony to mark his passage to manhood. Most Native American tribes held ceremonies for both young men and women to signify that they had reached adulthood.

which several tribes celebrated. The festival included dances (such as the Jumping Dance and the White Deerskin Dance), *recitations*, displays of tools, and decorations. In most tribes, this was an extravagant and complicated affair, but the Wiyots kept it simple and did not hold it as often.

The Miwoks had two kinds of ceremonies: sacred and profane. Sacred dances were more formal. The dancers wore fancy clothing and worried that spirits would harm them if they didn't handle ceremonial items correctly. Profane dances (non-sacred) were meant for fun and could not bring harm to those involved.

As mentioned before, most Native American tribes put a lot of importance on vision quests during male puberty, as this marked the transition to adulthood. However, in many tribes in the west and southwest, the ceremonies surrounding female puberty were even more important. Girls were usually isolated at this time. The Serrano called the girl's ceremony "Waxan." This was the time for a girl to learn how to become a good wife. In Pomo tribes, girls would be restricted to a special hut and given specific instructions. Costanoan girls were confined to their homes at this time, and their diet was limited. The Cahto ceremony lasted for six days, and afterwards, girls were expected to behave calmly and quietly for the next five months.

The Achumawi tradition was different—their girls were not expected to hide away. Instead, they had a feast with the rest of the tribe for 10 days. The next month, they would have another

celebration for nine days. Each month afterwards, they would have another celebration, each lasting one day less than the last. On the tenth month, the ritual was over and the girl was officially considered a woman. In these California tribes, girls usually got married soon after puberty (sometimes even before puberty), and her parents often chose her husband.

The Apache ceremony for female puberty was known as the Sunrise Ceremony (or *na'ii'ees*) and lasted four days. Girls would be covered in a mix of cornmeal and clay. They would dance and run in all four directions and feel the spirit of White Painted Woman. According to their legend, White Painted Woman was the first woman. She survived the Great Flood by floating in a shell, and her two sons saved the tribe from their enemy, Owl Man Giant. When she was an old woman, she met her younger self and merged with her so she could become young again.

The ceremony is still held today, but only about one-third of all Apache girls celebrate, and ceremonies don't always last four days anymore. Part of the reason is that it is so expensive. The total cost averages about $10,000. Several people must be paid, including the medicine man, the sponsoring godmother, and the dancers. The family must also pay for food for the whole community and the elaborate regalia.

In Serrano ceremonies for male puberty, boys would drink a **hallucinogen** made from the jimsonweed to give them "visions," then dance around a fire and learn songs. Afterwards, there was a feast and gift giving. In many tribes, the boys' noses would be pierced, and they were expected to go on vision quests.

Like other tribes, those in the Great Basin area thought bears represented special power. They had a late winter Bear Dance to honor these animals. Basin tribes didn't have many ceremonies because they were more occupied with survival than celebration. However, they did have Round Dances once or twice a year. During a Round Dance, people held hands and circled around a tree or pole, giving thanks for antelope hunts, rabbit hunts, and harvests. Some tribes also held a Round Dance to encourage the salmon to come out and then another one to give thanks for their arrival.

The Southern Paiutes of the Great Basin had one more important ceremony. After a loved one died, mourners were not allowed to bathe until the annual Mourning Cry Ceremony. They washed themselves during this ceremony, ending the official mourning period.

The Apaches avoided bringing up the subject of death. They were so afraid of ghosts that they avoided funeral ceremonies as much as possible. Although they had a great respect for elderly people, once a person died, they wanted to get rid of the body as soon as possible. Sometimes, the face of a deceased person would be painted, but then the body would be buried quickly. If possible, they even asked people outside of the tribe to bury their dead for them.

The Hopi of Arizona had some of the most varied and complex ceremonies of all Native American tribes. Some of their ceremonies were masked and some weren't, and all of the important ceremonies lasted for nine days. They had ceremonies for rain, to honor corn, to remember their legends, to celebrate harvests, and more.

Males belonged to one or more ritual societies: warrior, rain, hunt, and medicine. The rain chief held an important role—it was his job to attract the Horned Water Serpent (snake). The snake was the focus of a special rain dance known as the Snake Dance. It was believed the snake represented the link between sky and earth, so they would ask the snake to get the sky to shower down on the earth.

> Children were given special kachina dolls at an early age. They were carved from wood, painted, and clothed. However, the dolls weren't for playing. They were meant to teach the children about spirituality.

The Powamu Festival was an important one for Hopi children. When they were young, they learned about "kachinas" (also spelled "katsinas"). Kachinas were spirits who lived in the World Below for half of the year, then inhabited the bodies of villagers for the other half of the year. Kachinas might be male or female spirits, but they could be animal spirits, too. The Hopi participants usually wore masks and assumed the persona of the kachinas. It was felt they assumed the power of the spirits during these months as well. They had special responsibilities. They would give gifts to children when they were good or punish them when they misbehaved. They also conversed with the gods on behalf of the villagers.

37

NATIVE AMERICAN LIFE

The eyes of this Hopi kachina doll represent rain clouds, while the lashes are rain. Hopi children believe the dolls contain spirits. Young members of the Hopi tribe are initiated into kachina societies when they are around eight years old.

During the Powamu Festival, children around age eight were initiated into kachina societies. The kachina chief would invite the children into the *kiva*, sing a song about the underworld, and bless the children by sprinkling them with water and touching them with ears of corn. Then, three evil-looking ogre kachinas came in, howling and moaning and carrying whips. They whipped the children lightly four times each and then whipped each other. The chief gave the children presents, and they went home to feast.

The next morning, the children prayed and were given new names. Finally, they were allowed to know the secret. The kachinas took off their masks and danced for the children, showing them that they were ordinary men. Now that they knew the secret identities of the kachinas, they were sworn never to tell. The boys might grow up to become kachina dancers themselves one day. ⑤

39

NATIVE AMERICAN LIFE

This Sioux drawing on bison hide depicts the Sun Dance, a religious festival that tested the endurance of the tribe's warriors. Young braves were not allowed to eat for several days. Then, shallow cuts were made in the skin over the

warrior's chest and sharpened sticks were pushed through the skin. Ropes were then attached to the sticks, and the young man was expected to hang suspended until the sticks tore through his flesh and released him, as this Frederic Remington illustration from 1890 shows. The warriors then sang and danced in a circle until all were completely exhausted; during this time each hoped to receive a vision.

The purpose of the ritual was to thank the spirit of the Sun for past favors, and to ask the Sun to protect the tribe. In some cases warriors performed the ritual for purification before going into battle.

41

Dancers from one of more than 700 Native American
tribes from Canada and the United States compete at the
annual Gathering of Nations Powwow. The event is the
largest powwow, or tribal gathering, in North America,
drawing more than 3,000 participants of all ages.
Powwows usually include competitive dancing, singing,
craft shows, and storytelling, as well as a chance for
members of different tribes to meet.

5 Central and South American Festivals

The Poncas started what we now call **powwows** (they called this gathering the *hethuska*). It began as a formal ceremony for the tribe to celebrate good fortune and happiness, like when a baby was born or when crops were bountiful. They shared the ritual of the dance with other tribes, and, in the 1920s, some tribes held powwows that other tribes could attend. It became known as the Grass Dance, and it was different from the traditional sacred native dances. This dance wasn't religious or spiritual—it was just dancing for the sake of dancing.

The term "powwow" comes from the Narragansett word "taupowaw." It means "a wise speaker." Powwows originally referred to people with special abilities; they performed in healing ceremonies, they interpreted dreams, and helped ensure success in battles. Over time, the name was applied to native festivals. Today, powwows are open to native and non-native visitors alike. Powwows are colorful, fun celebrations of Native American traditions and family that are held all over the country throughout the year. Powwows last for one weekend each, and usually include competitive dancing, singing, craft shows, storytelling, and great opportunities for Native Americans to mingle.

Many rituals had a more serious function than powwows, however.

> At a powwow, although most dances are only open to natives, everyone in attendance is encouraged to participate in the Round Dance. Anyone who wishes to dance should enter the circle from the east side.

The Plains Indians, who were primarily hunters, had an important ceremony to ward off battles. Horseback tribes followed the buffalo from place to place, and often found themselves running into competing tribes. To keep peace between tribes, all of the Plains tribes respected a tobacco ceremony. You may have heard about "peace pipes." This comes from the ritual of sharing tobacco from a carved stone bowl. It was a sign that tribes would respect a neutral ground and not fight with each other. Men often wore a beaded pipe bag as part of their regalia.

By the 1750s, almost every Plains tribe also celebrated a four-day festival known as the Sun Dance. (Different tribes called it different names. For example, the Ponca called it the Mystery Dance, and the Cheyenne called it the New Life Lodge.) If a member of the tribe had a dream about holding a Sun Dance, then he would be the leader of it. During this festival, there was dancing, singing, and drumming. It was meant to help communities and individuals gain supernatural power. The tribes built a Sun Dance medicine lodge, which looked sort of like the skeleton of a tent. There were no solid walls or material over the structure. Instead, there was a wooden pole in the middle (the "sun pole") with a buffalo head hung from it, and lots of poles connected to it to create the shape of the lodge. Branches and leaves would be piled up around

A calumet was a special pipe that was used in a tobacco ceremony. Calumets have been called "peace pipes," because tribal leaders often shared the pipe after they agreed to a treaty.

the structure to fill in the gaps. Sacred ceremonies were held inside.

During this event, young warriors would fast, dance, and pray. They were only allowed to sleep about an hour each day. Even though the drummers and singers were allowed to take breaks, the dancers could not, and they often passed out from heat exhaustion or dehydration. They were expected to keep going, however, so they did, dancing back and forth through the lodge while others watched.

Then, wooden skewers were pushed through the skin on the warriors' backs or chests, and they were attached to the sun pole by strips of rawhide. While others performed a Sun Dance, the warriors on the pole would tear their skin until they yanked themselves free

45

NATIVE AMERICAN LIFE

from the pole, proving their power and representing the way a warrior might break free from capture by an enemy. The other dancers were supposed to look straight at the sun while they danced. This kind of sacrifice was supposed to help the participants have spiritual visions and dreams. Today, most of the torturous elements of ceremonies like this have been removed.

The Pawnees had a similarly brutal ceremony. In the Captive Girl Sacrifice (also known as the Morning Star Sacrifice), the tribe's warriors would kidnap a young girl from an enemy tribe. For four days, they would take her into the village and treat her well. Then they would put her in a special robe, paint her body half-black and half-red, tie her to a wooden frame, and shoot her in the heart with arrows. Her blood would drip onto buffalo meat that the people would then eat, and a warrior would paint his face with her blood. They believed this killing would help ensure they had good crops and special power from the forces of nature. In 1816, a man named Petalesharo, the son of the tribe's chief, cut the girl free just before she would have been killed. The practice of this ceremony ended soon after.

However, most ceremonies were not this violent. Cheyenne women had a *quilling* society with its own ceremonies. There were different levels of membership, based on what kinds of items a member had learned to craft. A beginner might only know how to make moccasins, while a more advanced member could make buffalo robes, back rests, and other items. When a member was promoted to a new level, she invited all the members of that level to a feast to celebrate her first new project. Each woman would share stories of the items they had quilled, and then a tribal member would come to witness the woman quilling her project. That witness would receive a gift. Then, members would offer prayers and eat.

Women were not allowed to participate in the Cheyenne Sacred Arrow Ceremony. Cheyennes believed that spirits had given their ancestors

Many people thought that Petalesharo should have been killed for letting the girl go, trading his life for hers. Instead, he was renamed Man Chief and later became chief of the tribe.

four sacred arrows on a mountain. The tribe had an arrow keeper, and he was the only person allowed to go into the lodge where the sacred arrows were kept in a bundle wrapped in animal hide. This keeper held his position for life.

When the tribe traveled, the arrow keeper held onto the arrows, and guards watched over him. The Sacred Arrow Ceremony was not held often. It was a secret ceremony designed to remove evil, for example, when a member of the tribe killed another member of the tribe. The ceremony was conducted for four days, and the village was quiet while fires burned. Only the males who were involved with the ritual were allowed to see or touch the arrows. If a woman looked at the arrows, the tribe believed she would die. ◐

47

NATIVE AMERICAN LIFE

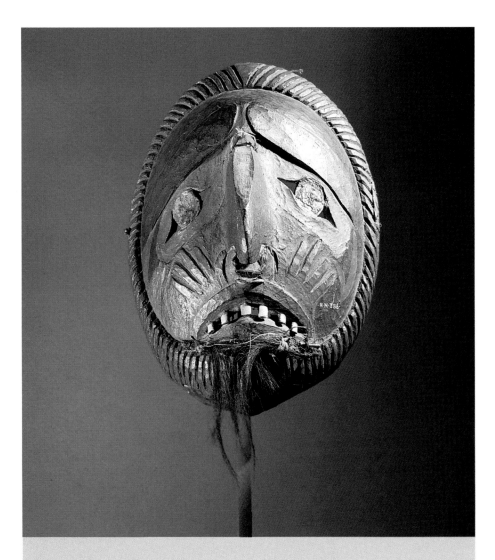

This mask was worn by *nutamat*, the Fool Dancer, during a sacred winter ceremony performed by the Kwakiutl tribe. The Fool Dancer was supposed to be violent and filthy. During the dance he threw stones and other objects at people who broke tribal rules.

Festivals of the North

In the northwest, Winter Spirit Dances were meant to help people stay in strong spirits throughout the cold, more isolated winter months. These ceremonies included lots of storytelling; the narrator would tell stories about the tribe's history or stories with lessons in them about improving lives. Sometimes, a story would be told over several nights.

The Kwakiutl of Vancouver Island, Canada, held a winter ceremony each year. Winter was the most sacred season, and the ceremony was announced by giving out red cedar bark ornaments. The Grizzly Bear Society would wear grizzly bear claws on their hands, or sometimes cover themselves with a whole bearskin. Grizzly Bear Dancers and the Fool Dancer (*nutamat*) worked together to make sure everyone behaved at this ceremony. The Grizzly Bear Dancer would intimidate participants with his power, and the Fool Dancer could attack people with sticks, stones, or even axes if he thought they weren't behaving properly.

The Fool Dancer hated cleanliness and often acted "crazy." While the other dancers moved one way, the Fool Dancer would move the opposite way. It was thought that the spirits who gave power to the Fool Dancer had long, runny noses, so whenever anyone mentioned anything about noses or smells, the Fool Dancer would throw a tantrum.

A new Cannibal Dancer (*hamatsa*) was selected each year. He had to live in the woods for a few months, and when he returned, he would bite people. According to legends, Cannibal Dancers would also eat skin from mummified bodies of slaves. By the end of the ceremony, he would return to normal, "healed" by the power of the ceremony.

There were a number of performances like this during the gathering. Throughout the ceremony, people would act out all different kinds of torture and violence, though most of it was not real.

During this ceremony, participants would often get new names, according to their job for the ceremony. In fact, they changed names repeatedly throughout their lives. If a chief died, his replacement would be given his name. Names were often given as gifts; for example, when a man got married, the wife's father would give the groom a new name.

The **potlatch** was an event that often followed ceremonies all around the northwest. A host would give a potlatch to show a change in his status or to erase shame. The potlatch usually consisted of speeches and a feast (or feasts), and always included gift giving. Guests would receive piles of gifts—pieces of the host's property. If they accepted them, the host would know they had accepted his change in status or accepted his "payment" for an embarrassment.

These potlatches were often so extravagant that a chief would be left poor afterwards. They didn't just do this to be generous, however.

A group of Ojibwa braves perform a Snow Shoe Dance in this drawing by George Catlin. The dance was intended to thank the Great Spirit for the first fall of snow.

This painting by George Catlin shows the interior of a Native American sweat lodge during a ceremony. The sweat lodge was used by the Indians to cleanse both their bodies and souls.

Potlatches were often meant for "showing off" and proving one's wealth. Rival chiefs would invite each other to potlatches as a challenge. At the end, they would know who was the wealthier chief because the other would be left with nothing!

Memorial potlatches lasted for several days and had two main purposes: to honor the dead and to help repair homes in the village. The chief's wife would ask relatives for donations of belongings and time, and during the ceremony, they'd repair homes in the village (including the chief's). At the end, the chief would give gifts to those who helped, although the gifts usually included items they had given as donations at the start of the ceremony.

> **"Eskimo" is a Cree word that means "eater of raw meat." Most Native Americans prefer the term "Inuit," which means "people who are alive at this time."**

Starting around the 1820s, Catholic priests began **missions** in the Plateau region. They thought it was important that they teach the Native Americans about their ways and to "enlighten" them. As part of that teaching, they insisted that the natives stop all of their dancing and ceremonies. This attempted **ban** spread throughout many Native American communities, but, in general, the natives responded by having even more frequent and extravagant ceremonies and potlatches.

At the end of the year in the Arctic, the Bering Sea Yupik had a ceremony known as the Bladder Festival. They believed every animal

53

had a soul and that every animal should be treated with respect and reverence. When they hunted seals in spring and summer, they saved the animals' swim bladders because they believed that when the animal died, its spirit went into its bladder. At the ceremony, they inflated the bladders and hung them up in the back of the **kashim**. Villagers sang, danced, and feasted, honoring the spirit of the seals. Finally, they brought the bladders to the ocean, deflated them, and sunk them beneath the waves. They believed these spirits would be born again as new seals the following year.

Tribes in northern Alaska had a special ceremony when the first whale was captured each season. Normal whale hunting couldn't begin until the ceremony was over. Whale hunting was dangerous, so every time a boat crew came back from a successful trip, it was cause for celebration. One of the customs that is still practiced today is a game that works like a human-powered trampoline. When the men came back, they would all stretch out a big piece of walrus hide and one man would stand in the middle of it. Then, the men would lift up the hide and throw the man up into the air. He would try to land on his feet, but this could be difficult when the men threw him too high.

Tribes in the Plateau area had many interesting ceremonies. During Blanket Ceremonies, people would gather in a *tepee*, or house, where a blanket blocked the entrance. The room would be dark and smoky, and people offered tobacco and sang to the spirits to invite them in. Leaders used this ceremony to ask questions of the spirits and to ask for help.

They also had Weather Dances (also known as Chinook Dances). You've probably heard of those; it's when a tribe would dance to ask the spirits to bring rain or melt the snow.

> **A whole tribe could live for a year off the meat of just two to four whales.**

Blue Jay Dances were opportunities to gain supernatural power. At night, these dancers would try to become like blue jays, which they thought had sacred powers. They might use this power to cure or to predict the future.

Like other tribes, the Kutenai also had sweat lodge ceremonies. These are still held throughout the country today and can be dangerous to those who aren't properly trained, because it can cause dehydration and hyperventilation. Inside the sweat lodge, men and women pray and try to purify themselves. Sometimes, they take breaks to swim in cold lakes or streams.

The Blackfoot of Alberta (Canada) and Montana had a Sun Dance similar to other Plains Indians, but with one important difference: a woman led the ceremony. For the first four days, the camp moved each day. On the fifth day, they built a medicine lodge. On the sixth day, they danced, blew whistles, and practiced self-torture. For the last four days, the men's societies would perform rituals. §

55

NATIVE AMERICAN LIFE

Chronology

1520s Spanish conquistadors and priests in the New World put an end to many of the ritual practices of the Aztecs and other native groups living in Mexico and Central America. In particular, human sacrifice is banned.

1769 The Spaniards begin establishing missions in California, where they hope to teach the natives of the region about Christianity.

1799 A Seneca chief named Handsome Lake begins to have visions. His teachings, based on these visions, are the basis of what becomes the Handsome Lake Church (also called the longhouse church).

1824 The Russian Orthodox Church begins missionary work in Alaska.

1830s The government of the United States begins a policy of removing Native American tribes from the south to new lands in Oklahoma. The Five Civilized Tribes (Cherokees, Seminoles, Creeks, Choctaws and Chickasaws) are moved along the "Trail of Tears."

1816 Petalesharo sets the enemy girl free during the Pawnee Captive Girl Sacrifice, thus ending this ceremony.

1870s The Chippewa Drum Dance begins; many hope it will bring peace between natives and non-natives.

1883 Soldiers ban an important ceremonial drink, so the Chiricahua leave the San Carlos Reservation in southern Arizona.

1890s The Ghost Dance becomes popular among Plains Indians; U.S. soldiers kill over 200 Sioux Indians preparing for a Sun Dance at Wounded Knee, South Dakota.

1910 The federal government outlaws the Sun Dance among Plains Indians because of its torturous elements.

1918 The Native American Church is founded in Oklahoma.

1920s Powwows gain popularity and become intertribal.

1959 Alaska becomes part of the United States, adding over 42,000 Native Americans to the population.

1970s The National Eagle Repository is established to provide eagle feathers for native ceremonies and regalia.

1976 The last Natchez ceremony is held.

1978 The American Indian Religious Freedom Act is passed.

1990 The Native American Graves Protection and Repatriation Act is passed, protecting native grave sites and demanding the return of bones and ceremonial artifacts to tribes.

2002 More than 700 tribes participate in the 19th annual Gathering of Nations powwow, the largest tribal gathering held in North America.

2003 According to the most recent U.S. Census, there are more than 2.5 million Native Americans living in the United States.

Glossary

ban a prohibition on something.

conch a large, spiral shell from a marine snail.

condolence an expression of sympathy.

fast to go without food for a period of time.

hallucinogen a substance that causes a person to see or hear things that aren't really there.

kashim the house used by Yupik men's societies.

kiva an underground room believed by Pueblos to be a doorway to the world of their native ancestors.

lacrosse a game in which players use a long-handled stick that has a mesh pouch at the end for catching, carrying, and throwing the ball at a goal.

mission a religious ministry established to covert the natives, usually to Christianity.

potlatch an extravagant feast, including abundant gift giving and prayer.

powwow Native American festivals that are held all over the country and open to all people.

quill to pierce something (usually fabric) with a hollowed-out feather.

recitation the act of reading or repeating something aloud, usually in public.

regalia special clothing, usually for a ceremony.

revere to worship.

shaman a healer or holy man or woman.

status the rank or place of a person or family within their tribe.

tepee made of buffalo skin, this was a "portable home" for Plains Indians because it was easy to transport and assemble.

Further Reading

Hoxie, Frederick E. *Encyclopedia of the North American Indians.* New York: Houghton Mifflin, 1996.

Moulton, Candy. *Everyday Life Among the American Indians.* Cincinnati: Writer's Digest Books, 2001.

Pennington, Daniel. *Itse Selu: Cherokee Harvest Festival.* Watertown: Charlesbridge Publishing, 1994.

Pritzker, Barry M. *A Native American Encyclopedia: History, Culture, and Peoples.* New York: Oxford University Press, 2000.

Staeger, Rob. *Native American Religions.* Philadelphia: Mason Crest Publishers, 2003.

Walker, Bryce and Jill Maynard, editors. *Through Indian Eyes.* Pleasantville: Reader's Digest, 1995.

Wilson, Mike. *Broken Promises: The U.S. Government and Native Americans in the 19th Century.* Philadelphia: Mason Crest Publishers, 2003.

Internet Resources

http://www.si.edu/resource/faq/nmai/start.htm

This site contains fascinating information collected by the Smithsonian Institution about Native American history and culture.

http://www.ilt.columbia.edu/k12/naha/natime.html

This is a timeline of Native American history and includes information on various events.

http://www.ahs.uwaterloo.ca/~museum/

The Elliott Avedon Museum and Archive of Games contains information on several games played by the Native Americans.

http://www.nativetech.org/games/

This site contains information on Native American culture and art.

http://www.csp.org/communities/docs/fikes-nac_history.html

The site provides a brief history of the Native American Church.

NATIVE AMERICAN LIFE

Index

Achumawi, 34
Acorn Ceremony, 32
Alaska, 54
Alberta, 55
Algonquians, 19, 21
Apache, 35, 36
Arctic, 53
Ashinabe, 19, 21

Bean Ceremony, 16
Bear Dance, 36
Bering Sea Yupik, 53
Big Heads, 15
Big House Ceremony, 21
Black Drink Ceremony, 23
Blackfoot, 55
Bladder Festival, 53
Blanket Ceremony, 54
Blessing Way Ceremony, 31–32
Blue Jay Dance, 55
Bowl Game, 16
Brush Ceremony, 32
Buzzard Men, 29

Cahto, 34
California, 32, 35
Canada, 49
Cannibal Dancer, 50
Captive Girl Sacrifice (Morning Star
    Sacrifice), 46
Catholic, 53
Cayuga, 15, 16
Cherokee, 23, 24
Cheyenne, 44, 46
Cheyenne Sacred Arrow Ceremony, 47
Chickasaw, 27
Chitimachas, 29
Choctaw, 23, 27, 28
Costanoan, 34
Creek, 23, 27

Dance of the Fire, 18
Delaware, 21

Enemy Way Ceremony, 32
European, 28

Fall Bread Dance, 21

False Face Society, 18
Feast of the Dead, 18–19
Feather Dance, 16
Fool Dancer, 49–50
Four Sacred Rituals, 16
Fox, 18

Ghost Dance, 32
Grass Dance, 43
Grease Drinking Ceremony, 21
Great Spirit, 27
Green Corn Ceremony (Busk), 10, 15, 16,
    23–24
Grizzly Bear Dancers, 49
Grizzly Bear Society, 49

Halloween, 15
Hopi, 36, 37
Horned Water Serpent, 37
Hupas, 32

Illinois, 16, 18
Iowa, 18
Iroquois, 15, 16, 21

Jumping Dance, 34

Kansas, 16
Kickapoo, 16
Kutenai, 55
Kwakiutl, 49

Lenni Len'pe, 21

Maple Ceremony, 16
Medicine Bundle, 24
Michigan, 16
Micmac, 21
Midewiwin (Medicine Dance), 19
Midsummer Ceremony, 29
Midwinter Ceremony, 15
Miwok, 34
Mohawk, 15
Montana, 55
Moon Ceremony, 16
Mourning Cry Ceremony, 36

Narragansett, 19, 43
Natchez, 28
Navajo, 31

NATIVE AMERICAN LIFE

New Mexico, 31

Ohio, 16
Oneida, 15
Onondaga, 15
Ontario, 19
Owl Man Giant, 35

Paiute, 36
Pawnees, 46
Personal Chant, 16
Petalesharo, 46
Plains tribes, 44, 55
Pomo, 34
Poncas, 43, 44
Powamu Festival, 37–39

Quebec, 19, 21

Rhode Island, 19
Round Dance, 36

St. Lawrence River Valley, 18
Seminole, 24
Seneca, 15
Serrano, 34–35
Shakalo Festival, 31
Shawnee, 21

Snake Dance, 37
Spring Bread Dance, 21
Strawberry Ceremony, 16
Sun Ceremony, 16
Sun Dance (Mystery Dance, New Life
    Lodge), 40–41, 44–46, 55
Sunrise Ceremony, 35

Thanksgiving Dance, 16
Thunder Ceremony, 16
Tuscaroras, 29

Vancouver Island, 49
Victory Dance, 32

War Dance, 21
Waxan, 34
Weather Dance (Chinook Dance), 55
White Deerskin Dance, 34
White Painted Woman, 35
Winter Spirit Dance, 49
Wisconsin, 16, 18
Wiyot, 32
World Renewal Festival, 32
Wyandotte, 18

Zuñi, 31

63

Picture Credits

NATIVE AMERICAN LIFE

Contributors

Dr. Troy Johnson is a Professor of American Indian Studies and History at California State University, Long Beach, California. He is an internationally published author and is the author, co-author, or editor of fifteen books, including *Contemporary Political Issues of the American Indian* (1999), *Red Power: The American Indians' Fight for Freedom* (1999), *American Indian Activism: Alcatraz to the Longest Walk* (1997), and *The Occupation of Alcatraz Island: Indian Self-Determination and the Rise of Indian Activism* (1996). He has published numerous scholarly articles, has spoken at conferences across the United States, and is a member of the editorial board of the journals *American Indian Culture and Research* and *The History Teacher*. Dr. Johnson has served as president of the Society of History Education since 2001. He has been profiled in *Reference Encyclopedia of the American Indian* (2000) and *Directory of American Scholars* (2000). He has won awards for his permanent exhibit at Alcatraz Island; he also was named Most Valuable Professor of the Year by California State University, Long Beach, in 1997. He served as associate director and historical consultant on the PBS documentary film *Alcatraz Is Not an Island* (1999), which won first prize at the 26th annual American Indian Film Festival and was screened at the Sundance Film Festival in 2001. Dr. Johnson lives in Long Beach, California.

Jenna Glatzer is a writer and the editor-in-chief of Absolute Write (www.absolutewrite.com), a Web site for writers. She has written for hundreds of national and online publications, recently including Salon.com and Writer's Digest. She is also the author of *The More Than Any Human Being Needs to Know about Freelance Writing Workbook* (Booklocker.com, 2000).